One Day in the Life of
THE NORTH-WEST

A collection of photographs by the people of the region
Written by Granada TV's Bob Smithies

Carnegie Publishing, 1991

One Day in the Life of the North-West
A collection of photographs by the people of the region

Captions and introduction by Bob Smithies

Published by Carnegie Publishing Ltd., 18 Maynard Street, Preston PR2 2AL.
Typeset in Plantin and News Gothic by Carnegie Publishing Ltd.
Printed by Pindar Graphics (Preston) Ltd., 1 Garstang Road, Preston

First published, November 1991

British Library Cataloguing-in-Publication Data
A CIP catalogue record for this book is available from the British Library

ISBN 0-948789-80-8

One Day in the Life of
THE NORTH-WEST

A collection of photographs by the people of the region

With an introduction and captions by Bob Smithies

Foreword

THE photograph album freezes the poignant and celebratory moments of every family's history. *One Day in the Life of the North-West* does the same – for an area of the country which is rich in the variety of its landscape and its character.

Wry, humorous, mischievous, irreverant, eccentric, are just a few descriptions of the people of the North-West – an area stretching from the Cheshire plains through the industrial belt of mid-Lancashire to the Trough of Bowland and the hills of the Lake District.

Granada, as the television contractor for the region for thirty-five years, has been in a unique position to observe its everyday life. This book captures a moment in its history – one day in May 1991 – which will evoke memories for generations to come.

David Plowright

Chairman, Granada Television

Introduction

GRANADA TONIGHT's producers lead dual lives. Meet them when their programmes have become memories and they are delightful, full of bonhomie and wit and always ready to accept one's offer of a drink. It is a different matter when they are at work. There they become remote and twitchy taskmasters who retreat into a neurotic preoccupation with the task of filling up thirty empty minutes, against the tyranny of the deadline. Come what may, Monday to Friday, *Granada Tonight* must be transmitted at six-thirty pm. It is the producer's job to fill every programme with the news of the day's events; with background material to the region's concerns; with items to make you ponder, sympathise, smile and – above all – continue to watch. Not everyone is cut out to be a producer. Some depart early for the limbo of industrial video-making; but others thrive on the combination of adrenalin and tension. They have a formidable task and its completion depends on the ability to hold on to their bottle, and to have a constant flow of ideas.

Everyone working on *Granada Tonight* contributes to the programme. The whole staff attends a conference every morning to discuss ideas for the day and, every now and then, when he is bored with my constant suggestion of a nightly series on the food and drink of France, our editor, John Huntley, takes his team of producers and news editors away for a brainstorming weekend in some country hotel. There, I am told, inspired by *haute cuisine*, fine wines and *en suite* facilities, they dream up long-term schemes to fill up empty spaces and keep our ratings higher than the opposition's. You might expect to find a degree of cynicism about the value of such gatherings in those of us who are not invited. Not in me you won't. After they met last February, John Huntley's think-tank came up with a cracker; and I couldn't begrudge them the odd salmon butty when I learned that the great idea pivoted on me.

It takes a lot to get me interested in photography. I was involved in it for twenty-four years and, when I ceased to be a *Guardian* staff photographer in 1974, that was it. I was quite proud of the pictures I had left behind in the paper's files, but I had had enough, and Granada offered different challenges. That's what I thought; but Granada depends upon individuals' expertise so, whenever any item with a photographic connection has appeared on the diary, I have copped for it.

So there I was in our Lancaster news centre, idly solving *The Times* crossword, when the call came from Jeff Anderson, a producer fresh from the think-tank's weekend away. He had this wonderful idea. It had been done before, of course. Great photographers had been hired to illustrate days in the lives of Rome, Paris and Rio de Janeiro; but I'd never heard of ordinary people being asked to picture their own region for themselves on one ordinary working day. I was hooked, and said so. 'Good', said Jeff, 'I'll leave you to get on with it, then'.

We decided to give the viewers around six weeks to prepare for a competition of which the best 100 entries would form an exhibition to tour the region. Those six weeks would be taken up with announcing and promoting it. We would call it 'One Day in the Life of the North-West'; but which day? Thursday evenings were scheduled for lengthy items about the competition in *Granada Tonight* and it was up to me to make those items. That was no problem, but suppose we announced the big day only to have it overshadowed by national events? There was a whiff of a General Election in the air. John Major was thought to be going for the kill. Thursdays are a popular day for elections. Our Political Correspondent, Jim Hancock, was consulted. We opted to let loose the cameras of the North-West on Thursday, May 23rd.

The announcement was made in *Granada Tonight* on Thursday April 11. I recorded it in Garstang. It was market day there, which provided a lively Lancashire background. The item comprised some six 'pieces to camera', each separated by a short sequence of still pictures of the market with the sound of a camera shutter going off with every change of photograph. At the end of each piece to camera, in which I gave the viewers the background to 'One Day in the Life of the North-West', I lifted my camera; but I did not take any pictures. That was left to our cameraman, Barry Wilkinson. After I had done my bits he wandered around the market for half an hour with his television camera. The pictures that appeared were freeze-frames from his tape.

The item worked. After the programme the switchboards of our five news centres were swamped with enquiries: 'What are the rules?'; 'How many pictures are we allowed to enter?'; 'Can we take pictures in black and white?'. We assured callers that all would be revealed in plenty of time. There was a call to my Lancaster office from John Huntley: 'You will be organising the touring exhibition, won't you Bob?' Helpppppp!!!!!

Help arrived in the form of Nakib Narat, the researcher-journalist on the strength at my Lancaster news centre. He looked for about a dozen venues initially, but in the end it went to thirteen. He had to negotiate with council officers and to inspect halls, libraries and museums. Newspaper coverage had to be organised through Granada's Press Officer, Clare Walker. There had to be budget consultations with our General Manager, Geoff Rowe. Nakib had to arrange the on-screen appearances of the best and most varied professional photographers in the North-West. He had plenty to do.

Every Thursday evening for five weeks, *Granada Tonight* kept the competition in the minds of our viewers. We reiterated the theme; then, to inspire the entrants to great things, we featured the work and methods of those top professionals. At their gallery in the Cumbrian village of Dent, I interviewed John and Eileen Forder, who portray the hard lives of the people of the Dales and the Lakeland fells in sympathetic and superbly

produced books. At his home in Liverpool, the great sports photographer Steve Hale told me how he took the split-second action shots which had brought him international acclaim.

John Cocks, the staff photographer of *Lancashire Life* and *Cheshire Life*, allowed us to accompany him on assignment. We met him in deepest rural Cheshire, where he was photographing Joyce Dalton, celebrated breeder of Angora goats. What a patient woman she is! She sat calmly in her barn, surrounded by bleating goats, hot lights, a television crew and various relatives and colleagues, while I tried to interview John Cocks as he tried to photograph Joyce. Throughout, heavy rain did its best to ruin David Brown's soundtrack. I have never seen David so close to tears.

I interviewed Clement Cooper in a Manchester wine bar. He was taking portraits of a young model at the start of a new book about women. Clement is young, intense and totally uncompromising about his work. His last book was a remarkable study of Manchester's ethnic communities. Instead of the usual concentration on racial problems and inner-city tensions, Clement Cooper showed us the faces of ordinary people leading their ordinary lives; beautiful pictures of people who were sad, happy, angry, tired, vivacious, cunning or artless.

Gary Talbot, on the other hand, showed us the faces of people as they like to be seen. Gary is one of the most successful portrait photographers in the world. He comes from a family of press photographers, but he found the diary assignments at the *Daily Mail* frustrating. He went off to play professional football for Chester and Crewe Alexandra, scored the fastest hat-trick of goals in an FA cup tie and then returned to photography. He now travels the globe to portray princes, potentates and politicians, and produces stunning pictures of clients who come to his elegant studios in Chester.

At that point, after such a plethora of inspirational advice, and with only a week to go to May 23rd, I reckoned the North-West's camera carriers would be enthused and ready for the off. Some couldn't wait! We started to get entries before we asked for them. One woman sent me a snap of the outside of her newly-decorated bungalow. There was a pretty shot of a Cornish cove taken in 1979. There were more than enough shots of what is popularly known as 'mooning'; then there was the body-builder. He sent us a picture of himself, posing precariously on one knee on a card table in turquoise briefs. It wasn't a bad picture but, apart from disqualification for being submitted three weeks early, he had ruined the print by folding it neatly into four to get it into his pink envelope.

In May 22nd's *Granada Tonight* I repeated the competition's rules, and told the viewers they would have almost twenty-four hours to take pictures from one second after midnight. Then I went home, downed a very large tranquillising scotch and crossed my fingers.

Jeff Anderson was producing *Granada Tonight* on Thursday May 23rd and he was not short of ideas. The day was full of hard, regional news. Hospital patients who had contracted the HIV virus from NHS blood were fighting for compensation. Michael Heseltine was about to tell the North-West cities that they would have to compete for cash from White-hall. Stan Mortenson had died, and my Lancaster colleague Paul Crone was booked to compile a tribute to the legend of Blackpool soccer. In Belgium fifty kilos of cannibis were found in the car of two Merseyside men. There was a £30,000 wages snatch at Little Hulton. The village of Ribchester was accused of having a sour-puss attitude towards its tourists. Lancashire were facing Surrey in the County Cricket Champion-ship, and I wanted five television crews deployed around the whole of Granada-land to see the region's photographers capturing One Day in the Life of the North-West. Even I had to see that I had to be joking. Five crews for one story?! I got 'em! By some weird alchemy known only to Daphne Hughes and Nicky Hargreaves on the Assignments Desk I was given the five crews. All of the other stories for the programme would be covered, but I would get my five crews for part of the day. Jeff Anderson had one question: 'Are you sure you'll find enough photo-graphers out on the streets?' Well, I didn't come up the Irwell on me Granny's piano, did I?! Of course I would! For days Nakib Narat had been telephoning camera clubs and college photographic courses to make sure that we would find enough photographers. And we did.

I took the Lancaster crew to Fleetwood, where Chairman Bob Stead and a dozen members of his local camera club were seeking

inspiration amid the yachting fraternity in the town's new marina. Carl Hawkins emerged from the gentlemen's-club-like surroundings of our Chester news centre to find a father and daughter team snapping away on the banks of the Dee. Andy Gill, that Rottweiler among news reporters, did a tender little piece with primary school children who were doing a photo-project on Ashton-Under-Lyne. In Blackburn, Rob McLoughlin, who leads a polymathic existence as co-producer of the programme and head of our Blackburn news centre, managed to put local college student photographers on tape while simultaneously covering Ribchester's alleged attitude to tourism. And in Liverpool, Bob Greaves found a confusing situation as the South Liverpool Photographic Society swooped down on the children of St Joseph's Primary School, who had come, innocently and unknowingly, from Wallasey for a city centre picnic.

Nakib Narat supervised the editing together of all that wonderful material and that evening we filled four minutes and twenty-seven seconds of *Granada Tonight*'s heavy schedule with the story of a unique event.

This is how the opening of *Granada Tonight* ran on the evening of May 23rd, 1991:

John Huntley to camera.

'Hello and welcome. Tonight, the hospital patients who contracted the HIV virus from NHS blood. The mother of a twelve-year-old victim tells of her fight for compensation.'

Bob Greaves to camera.

'Also tonight, the Government tells North-West cities they must compete for Whitehall cash. We look at hard-up areas which could lose out. Paul Crone pays tribute to Stan Mortensen, Blackpool legend.'

John Huntley to camera.

'And Bob Smithies puts us in the picture – how the region has gone camera-crazy for a day.'

The competition item was duly transmitted, and then I joined the programme down-the-line from Lancaster to recap on the rules and tell entrants they had a fortnight to process and submit their pictures. A fortnight! The first entrant delivered his prints, by hand, that night to the security man at Lancaster.

After the weekend the flow became a torrent and the slender frame of my secretary, Dawn Taylor, became encased in a mass of envelopes, parcels and block-mounted giant-sized enlargements. Rules? What rules? Lancaster's central post office had been given early warning and the mailroom staff here at Whitecross had to get used to hopping over an obstacle course of mailbags. Dawn had a truly monumental task. She logged every entry by name, address and telephone number. There were thousands, yet, throughout, the poor lass had to maintain her normal duties: sorting the petty cash; keeping in contact with reporters and crews on assignments; dealing with callers, both corporeal and telephonic; looking after interviewees for the programme. I felt obliged to help: I started to brew my own coffee.

We were getting some wonderful pictures in, I was delighted. On each of three successive Thursdays, Nakib Narat edited a pile of them to music. They were duly shown on *Granada Tonight*. There was no need for careful selection. Most of the entries were of excellent quality. It would be next to impossible to choose the best 100.

June 6th, the closing date, came. Dawn collapsed with a hysterical giggle of relief and the judges arrived; among them, John Huntley and Janet Hayman, who was replacing Jeff Anderson as the lead producer of *Granada Tonight*. No, the programme's pace hadn't proved too much for Jeff. He had been promoted to endure even greater amounts of adrenalin and tension for *World in Action*.

The judges had a number of criteria to consider. There had to be a spread of pictures across the region and throughout the twenty-four hours of May 23rd. We were not judging on technical or artistic excellence. This was not to be an elitist collection of exquisite photographs. The winning 100 pictures must reflect the way the ordinary people of the North-West had responded so magnificently to our call for their portrayals of their home ground. So a brilliant idea with technical imperfections had a better chance of success than a stunningly presented mediocrity. As it happened, the best 100 began to stand out from the thousands spread across the studio floor. The judges stood, stretched and congratulated themselves. Then I asked them to choose a further twenty.

That was wisdom born out of previous experience. Sure enough, after we had written to congratulate each winner, and ask them for their negatives to produce the exhibition prints, my caution was justified. A few winners never replied, and a few others telephoned us, as one man did in tears, 'I can't find my bloody negative'.

Granada Tonight transmitted the winning pictures over the two successive Thursday evenings in the June. On July 4th I opened our touring exhibition at Granada's headquarters in Manchester. It is a visual feast which combines the superb photo-printing skills of CPS Ltd., the elegant creativity of our designer, Don Stevens, and above all, to my great joy and relief, the wit, compassion, observation and obvious love for the region of our viewers.

A few days after the exhibition's opening I received a letter in the internal mail. The envelope bore that typeface which seems to be exclusive to executive suites and which can presage triumph or disaster. It was from Granada Television's Chairman, David Plowright: 'Congratulations on the idea and the exhibition. Have you thought of publishing a coffee-table glossy brochure?' Oh, haven't I just!

Bob Smithies

October 1991

The earliest of the day's winners is a Preston paradox: manual packet sorting in a Mechanised Letter Office? But just look at that fascinating spread of regional destinations.

SORTING OFFICE
Mr. M. P. Knowles, Walton-le-Dale

This is a fine photograph which combines excellent composition with highly skilled black and white technique. It is the boy's cheerful smile, though, that makes the picture a classic.

PAPER BOY
Eric Lancaster, Rochdale

An early bird has caught the early birds here, and captured a woman with a mission. The stick, the heavy bag and the warm clothing are the accroutrements of her age. Her face, though, is all youthful determination.

LYTHAM PARK
Lynn Parker, Newton-with-Scales

One day that magpie will push its luck too far. This picture shows intelligent anticipation and considerable skill in the use of the telephoto lens.

CONFRONTATION
Arthur Pilkington, Newton-le-Willows

08:45

Mr Birtill, former editor of the
Chorley Guardian, retired recently
after 29 years as Secretary of
Chorley Golf Club. This is the
'chuck-in,' when golfers put 25p each
in the kitty to turn the game into a
competition.

CHUCKING-IN
George Birtill, Chorley

09:00

Eunan submitted a large entry of
beautifully taken and well printed
pictures. They are worth a book on their
own. This one, though, says everything
about the allotment sub-culture of old
industrial Lancashire.

TYLDESLEY ALLOTMENTS
Eunan Jones, Atherton

A first-class piece of portraiture: it was taken on a long-defunct two-and-a-quarter-square-film-carrying-non-automation Microcord. Which proves that it's not cameras that make good pictures.

POSTMAN
M. T. Bentley, Littleborough

09:10

SCHOOLBOY
James Birchall, Rossendale

08:40

Here is the photographer's grandson leaving for school. His expression shows that this is an unposed picture; a picture which amply demonstrates why Mr Birchall has become an Associate of the Royal Photographic Society.

09:10

There are around forty faces in this picture yet the eye is drawn immediately to the two schoolgirls in the centre. It is a great photograph, and the subject admirably chosen to illustrate the daily life of the region.

SCHOOL ASSEMBLY
D. Birchall, Prestwich

09:20

This will probably appear in a hundred years' time in some book about 'Old Manchester'. The men are working on the city's new rapid transit system. There's good photography with historic value here.

ST. PETER'S SQUARE, MANCHESTER
J. Clayton, Warrington

13

 09:30

You know what they say about a watched kettle. This is a well-observed snapshot. We can see that this tradesman takes sterilised milk in his tea and that he improvises a seat out of anything. But why is he swinging that hammer?

 MY MATE'S BREAK
H. K. Cumpsty, Oldham

09:30

'Any day is washing day', says Mrs Vines, and you couldn't have a more mundane subject than this. But, with perfect composition, Mr Vines has turned ordinariness into beauty.

WASHING DAY
Albert Vines, Rawtenstall

09:30

Rajiv Gandhi was assassinated on May 22nd and this is a memorial service in Preston's Gujarat and Hindu Temple. Mr Ainsworth's opportunity came through tragedy, but he responded with good taste.

GANDHI MEMORIAL
D. Ainsworth, Hoghton

09:30

Preparing for net practice at Fairfield High School in Widnes: a classically balanced picture. But I am intrigued by those pads. How long have they been in use? They look as if Dr Grace might have passed them on!

PADDING UP
Paul Cousins, St. Helens

Oh, Susan, how could you? This goes to show that, to capture the great pictures of life, you simply have to ignore the tugging of the heart strings and get on with the job. I hope you gave him a cuddle afterwards.

TRAPPED

Susan Walsh, Chadderton

 DISPENSING
Doris Grose, Warrington

I have always wondered what goes on in the back room. Chemists' shops are a taken-for-granted part of our daily lives. Doris Grose has snapped the vital concentration that we take for granted in our pharmacists.

Again, an everyday subject has produced a winner, and the dreary time-consuming boredom of a post office pensions queue has been transformed by a well-caught and radiant smile.

 PENSION QUEUE
Lilian Malcolm, Blackpool

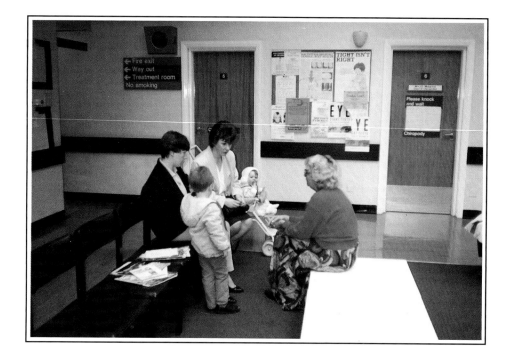

HEALTH CENTRE
Wendy Aldred, Blackburn

This epitomises good local services. In an anonymous-looking clinic, Wendy has found an oasis of reassurance and calmness. It is an everyday scene, but it needed an imaginative eye to record it.

Just look at the concentration on the two faces. Look, too, at the detail in the picture: the clothes brushes; the diploma; the razor blade dispenser. Even the mirror reflects part of the story. This is a valuable piece of social history – one day we'll see it as 'the way we were'.

SHORT-BACK-AND-SIDES
Malcolm Burley, New Brighton

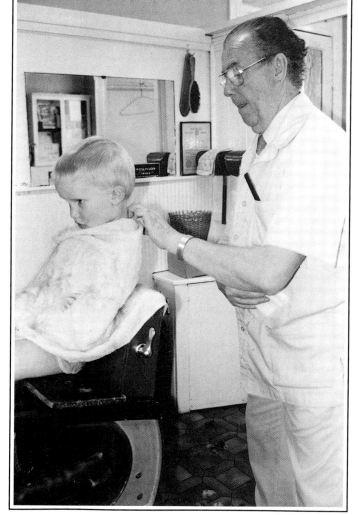

ORMSKIRK MARKET
Bill Hackney, Southport

Here is a cleverly isolated slice of life in the bustle of the market-place. There is tenderness here, as well as acute observation; and a nicely judged juxtaposition of wheelchair and babycart.

At first glance this is just a simple snapshot; but I love the woman's concentration on her task and the way she manages to find some physical comfort in a busy kitchen. Love the trainers!

SCHOOL KITCHEN
S. Gates, Southport

10:45

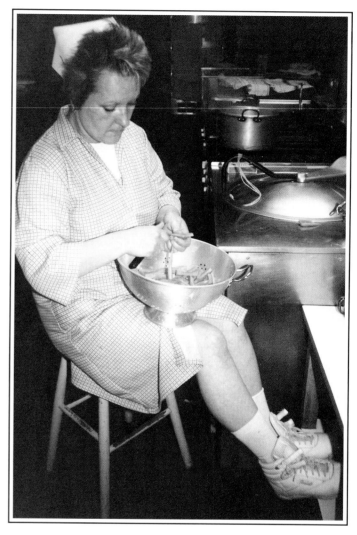

It is amazing what goes on on a Thursday morning. Here is an artist, totally absorbed in his work amid his raw material and the preserved bits of our heritage at Turton Tower. I wonder if Yasser Arafat has missed any headgear recently?

WOOD SCULPTOR
David Scrafton, Bolton

▲ CHESTER BUSKER
J. S. Millichamp, Rhyl

10:45

I think this busker enjoys his life. He is fastidious about his hair, he dresses to please himself. There is evident skill in his fingers; and his dog loves him. Pity the cap isn't a bit fuller, really.

What a beautifully composed picture this is. I have passed the shop in Lancaster a thousand times. Yet it took Ann Smith to photograph what had never occurred to me.

▼ FURNITURE MAN
Ann Smith, Lancaster

11:00

Mr Shaw doesn't tell us what the fire is about, but the man on the machine seems totally unconcerned, so that's all right. He is engaged on coastal protection works. It is an unusual and dramatic picture.

COASTAL PROTECTION
P. Shaw, Prestatyn

11:00

Here we are, preparing the meals at the WVS Dinner Centre in New Ferry, and with just few enough cooks to make an excellent broth. Nothing sexist about the WVS either – that man is doing sterling service.

W.V.S.
B. Catesby, Port Sunlight

This is one of the day's most important events: the delivery of ale in the wood from the local brewery. The drayman, whose girth suggests he enjoys his job, is displaying great accuracy. The horse is not expected to pull too heavy a load. I bet it's an excellent pint, too.

DRAYMAN
A. Coffey, New Mills

11:15

It is the leached-out moorland behind the drystone wall that says 'this is Rossendale'. He is a good farmer, too. The grass in the foreground is in good heart. The goats are in good condition as well. They're quite fond of each other, aren't they?

LAUND FARM
Paul Dootson, Reedsholme

POSTMAN'S DIRECTIONS
J. Labdon, St. Helens

He could be telling the postman how to find his way through Ormskirk, which is highly unlikely. Or he might be discussing the weather. Either way, the conversation piece has been cleverly isolated from a still recognisable background.

We had dozens of pictures from Ormskirk Market, and this is the only one which shows inactivity. Yet he is obviously a busy man. That brown shoelace must be a very temporary replacement.

ORMSKIRK MARKET
K. Ainsworth, Wigan

11:45

11:50

ELEPHANT WALK
Nigel Hillier, Kelsall

This is a remarkable picture by any standards. I mean, when did you last see an elephant walking through Chester? Nigel has also captured an unfortunate juxtaposition which I shall refrain from pointing out.

Nothing could be more typical of the Ribble estuary than this perfect composition in straight thirds. Everything seems to be placed laterally: the shrimpers, the tide and the boats. Even the light is flat.

SHRIMPERS
P. Simpson, Lytham

12:00

This could be nowhere else but Barrow-in-Furness. Whenever there is a story about the Vickers works, television invariably features the exodus of cyclists from the plant, and we are all familiar with the sight, Vic Rawlinson more than most. He worked there. And what's wrong with familiarity?

VICKERS BIKERS
Vic Rawlinson, Barrow

12:00

Accurate observation has transformed a simple snapshot into an amusing, even surreal comment on the house painter's lot. The ladder suggests regular professional use; but I'm sure the shoes and trousers are those of the DIY man.

DIY FEET
Karen Kershaw, Poynton

12:05

This is a study in red; the background, the boys' collars and the beakers make an eye-catching design. The picture is made, though, by the children's expressions.

SCHOOL LUNCH
Pauline Hughes, Blackpool

12:45

The temptation at a location like this is to go for a wide shot, to display the local landscape. This is the exception that proves the imaginative photographer's rule. The detail is delightful, and you can tell the boatman is an expert. Look at his stance and the way he stows his rope.

BUNBURY STAIRCASE
P. Critchley, Bebington

What a lovely study of childhood! This is a brilliantly composed picture, showing great skill. It also captures that childhood combination of uncertainty with experiment.

LIVERPOOL LUNCHEON
C. Douglas, Anfield

13:30

You can see it as soppy and sentimental, school of Mabel Lucy Attwell if you like. You can also see it as an excellently judged photograph. The girl hasn't quite kissed her friend, and the white space between their heads makes the composition perfect.

DEE BRIDGE KISS
Sandra Egerton, Saltney

BUILDING TRADES
Joe Fallon, Salford

I am reminded here of the Ragged Trousered Philanthropists. It was a good idea to bring all the building trades together on one site, and it is an idea superbly executed. This is another one for 21st-century historians.

 OLDSTERS,
BIRKENHEAD PARK

J. Steele, Birkenhead

Many of the competition's more expert entrants have stuck to black and white photography. Perhaps it is because they can control their results better. Certainly colour could not have improved this study of two men enjoying the fullness of their years.

13:35

13:36

Gina has produced a beautifully-lit study of a man at his hobby. As one whose tool kit comprises nothing but an axe and a wobbly-headed hammer, I am humbled by the condition of those immaculate chisels.

WOOD TURNING
Gina Rimmer, Southport

13:45

This is not a technically accomplished photograph. It has great value, though, because it is a witty record of one of the various activities that occur on any ordinary working day. It made me consider my own waistline, too!

KEEP FIT
Parveen Chowdhary, Rochdale

13:50

If this wasn't taken on a large format camera, I'll eat my Pentax. The portrait would be wonderful on any camera, but the fineness of detail, and the quality of the colour convinces me. Goodness – you can even see that it was taken at one-fifty p.m. and twenty seconds.

ONE MAN & HIS DOG – AND CAT
Keith Buckley, Mossley

14:15

14:00

ALBERT DOCK LOVERS
Steve Boardman, Eccles

A fine piece of contre-jour photography here: it is beautifully printed and presented. What makes the picture a winner, though, is the quality of tenderness and affection in the subjects.

Linda says she sought inspiration around Fulwood all morning. Then she found Malcolm Hendrick at the end of her street. He danced around a bit for her and, she says, asked her if his efforts were worth the price of a pint. I think the result is worth the price of a gallon.

SWEEPER
Linda Viney, Preston

33

14:10

Arnside is a lovely Victorian village on the shores of the Kent estuary in South Lakeland. They say that older people retire there to die, but then forget what they came for. It's the walking, the beauty and the bowls that keep them going, evidently.

ARNSIDE BOWLERS
Stuart Templar, Timperley

14:30

This picture appeals to me enormously. Here are four tough workmen whose postures are almost genteel. Perhaps it's the muted colour that softens their tattooed edges. It could almost be a Victorian tea-party.

TEA BREAK
W. P. Upton, Morecambe

My young colleague says this is the only bum shot in the book. I think it is simply funny. It also suggests quick thinking allied to acute observation.

 FLAGGER

Miss M. Amriding, Preston

14:30

Here is a newspaper seller with nothing to shout about. There isn't a newspaper in sight. Perhaps he is lubricating his larynx while waiting for the Liverpool Echo's next edition: a lovely portrait.

NEWSPAPER SELLER
J. Malone, Bootle

14:30

Sadly, this is an everyday scene in almost any city, and the picture shows hopelessness and despair. Mrs Jones has carefully avoided easy identification. These men retain some dignity.

DOWN AND OUT IN CHESTER
Mrs C. Jones, Wrexham

14:45

 LOST AT SEA
Mrs T. O'Shea, Liverpool

Did this happen to some stick-in-the-mud driver who left the centre lane of the M6? Or did a local joy-rider believe there was a short cut from West Kirkby to Flint? There's nothing at sea about the photography, though.

Sandra is a nurse at the Fylde Coast Hospital. She was allowed to take her camera into the operating theatre, where she captured an everyday moment of intense and vital concentration.

 EYE SURGERY
Sandra Pisani, Blackpool

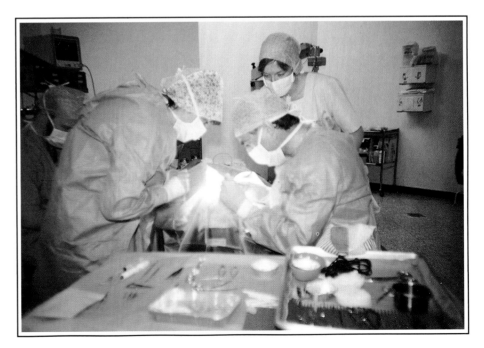

14:50

'G-Granville! C-Call that a f-flamin' w-w-watchdog?' The world of Arkwright and Nurse Gladys survives. This is the timeless North West, where the proud corner shop stands firm against the m-m-march of the h-h-hypermarkets.

OPEN ALL HOURS
Sue Briers, St. Helens

Dorothy Smith achieved her 100th birthday on May 23rd, in the Heliosa Nursing Home at Congleton. This was her party, and there was plenty of assistance there to blow out all those candles.

CENTENARIAN
Maggie Walker, Congleton

15:00

One of the most familiar scenes in the North West, and it is none the worse for that. Mr Seaman found plenty of nautical activity there, and had the sense to photograph it for our competition.

BRIDGEWATER CANAL
K. Seaman, Eccles

15:00

What an enchanting picture! Jodie Watkins and Jay Laycock are both thirteen months old, obvious friends and genuine water babies.

EARLY BATH
Ken Tomlinson, Morecambe

15:00

It won't win any prizes for sports photography, but Mr Calland's picture has all the atmosphere of Lancashire village cricket: well-turned-out players; a well-kept pitch; and the brooding moors beyond.

CRICKET MATCH
E. Calland, Milnrow

15:00

Even though he has 'Menace' embroidered on his vest, he isn't really, is he? As for the other fellow, he's about to hold hands with his girlfriend, so not much menace there. As Ben's picture shows, it is hard to be individualistic when you are forced to conform.

MANCHESTER PUNKS
Ben Lavelle, Swinton

15:00

A fine picture; the group is perfectly composed and isolated from the surroundings. John Powell has combined patience, anticipation and skill to capture a moment of maternal joy.

QUARTETTE
John Powell, Oldham

15:15

Nicely spotted, Peter! Here is a picture which proves that in even the most dedicated vocations there is room for the occasional moment of childlike pleasure.

BEACH SISTERS
Peter Cameron, Poulton

15:15

This is one of the pictures which has given me the greatest pleasure. Keith photographed one of the most ordinary of human activities. Yet his picture also tells us that this is a particularly proud mum. Look at how prettily the pram is fitted out. She is a credit to Lord Street.

FEEDING BABY –
SOUTHPORT
Keith Fisher, Crosby

15:30

A simple picture of one of life's simple pleasures. The group was photographed at Guy's Court in Bilsborrow, just off the A6 near Preston. It is a picture of friendship and pure enjoyment.

AFTERNOON TEA
P. F. Shardlow, Poulton

15:30

This is no Aussie soap. These are real neighbours; houseproud, fond of a good gossip and fonder still of a good cup of tea. It looks like a simple snapshot, but the facial expressions suggest that there is something serious under discussion.

NEIGHBOURS
Marion Key, Northwich

15:30

A Victorian open day at Woodlands School in Birkenhead: the girls are very much part of 1991, however. It is the central heating pipes that are truly Victorian.

VICTORIAN SCHOOL
G. W. Booth, Birkenhead

The essence of late spring is here. The flowers and leaves are positively rampant, and you can almost feel the heat in the sunshine.

SHROPSHIRE UNION
Alan Hughes, Winsford

Frankly this looks like the triumph of hope over experience. He's never going to get his rear end through that gap, and his mate doesn't think so either. The picture shows that at least Colin Hamilton knew what he was doing.

HEADING FOR TROUBLE
Colin Hamilton, Kirkby

15:45

An important moment in the history of St Ambrose Barlow School in Netherton. The picture shows the opening of their new Resource Centre, and I hope they have the resources, after providing that appetising spread, to fill it.

◄ RESOURCE CENTRE
Graham Taylor, Southport

15:45

This was taken up near Ingleton, in the limestone country of the north of our region, where life is tough and a good pair of working dogs is as important as a reliable tractor.

TOW SCAR ROUND-UP
John Brown, Ingleton

PROMENADERS
Margaret Salisbury, Prestatyn

Margaret lectures in photography and her expertise shines through this scene on Prestatyn's new coastal defences. Pity there wasn't one more hard hat for perfect balance but it is still a great picture.

The head gamekeeper, John Blude, poached an excellent shot here. His assistant is returning home after feeding the laying stock in the woods at Silverdale. And those yellow buckets transform the scene.

GAMEKEEPER
John Blude, Silverdale

46

16:05

There is highly skilled photography here. Fred could have photographed the man unawares, but his expression for the camera is telling. He is beautifully isolated from the background and the composition is first class.

STREET MACHINE
Fred Ritchie, Swinton

16:10

Peter Cameron has given us two winners from Blackpool in this competition. After the ice-cream eating sisters on the beach, he dashed into the Tower to remind us that, in Blackpool, some things never change.

TOWER BALLROOM
Peter Cameron, Poulton

47

It is the angle of the shot and the thatcher's dynamic posture that make this a good picture. At least I think he's a thatcher. He might be a demolition man using karate to deal with a dodgy chimney!

 WILMSLOW THATCHER
Janet Smirles, Woodford

16:45

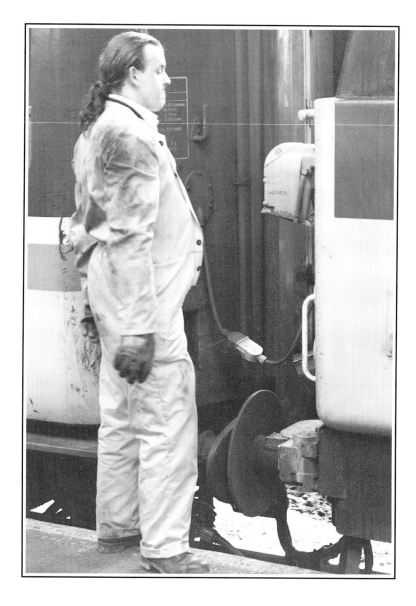

 PLATFORM 3
Grenville Hartley, Horwich

16:45

If it was not for the hairstyle, this Preston railwayman could have been photographed any time during the last century. There is a traditional pride in his stance, and his expression shows he is used to judging things to a nicety.

17:00

LABOUR OF LOVE
Jean Speak, Great Harwood

Nothing in this picture is superfluous. It is quite perfect, and says all there is to be said about anonymous, hardworking dedication in the back streets of the North West. That bucket has seen out a few mops too.

Henri Cartier-Bresson's technique has served David Coggins well. Like the French master, he chose his spot, waited and, sure enough, something happened, in this case the arrival of the mantra chanters to transform a prosaic scene into poetry.

HARE KRISHNA
David Coggins, Blackburn

17:00

17:00

I know there is nothing to fear. I know that modern dentistry is painless. So why does this picture send a shiver of terror through me. I'm sure the young patient isn't scared – I mean it's just a normal everyday occurrence, isn't it?

BOLTON DENTIST
Rev. Cliff Fane, Little Lever

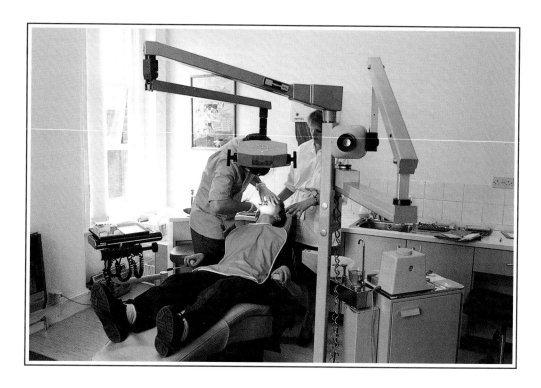

17:10

Belinda's picture shows that cone disease has now spread from the motorways to the trunk roads. The road has been widened, too. I am sure there used to be a separate cycle track there when I was a lad. Progress??

EAST LANCS. ROAD
Belinda Hastie, Worsley

50

The aged, blind and disabled of Bacup have enjoyed this annual treat since 1953 – Coronation year. The town's workers contribute a penny a week to pay for it. After they had spent an afternoon in Fleetwood, Karen caught up with the trippers at high tea back in Bacup.

ANNUAL TREAT

Karen Spencer, Bacup

17:45

Mr Hardman shows that if you walk home from work carrying a camera, as he does, you will have plenty of photo-opportunities. I am also assured that the canal is only some four inches deep here. What worries me are those bread pallets. What baker can afford to lose 32 of those?

ROCHDALE CANAL

J. Hardman, Moston

51

PLAYTIME
John Bulger, Rawtenstall

What a happy picture! John Bulger has caught the action perfectly; and he has used the evening light with great skill.

Barbara photographed her joggers on the Otterspool Promenade in Liverpool. She is obviously a dedicated photographer. She tells me that she used a Minolta Dynax camera with a 300mm telephoto lens, giving an exposure of one seven hundred and fiftieth of a second on XP2 film. So there.

JOGGERS
Barbara Dawson, Tarbock Green

17:30

18:12

18:30

This is one of the most perfect portraits in the entry. It has critically sharp definition, a perfect balance of colours – and the most delightful expression from the boy. Lovely picture.

TREED
D. A. Thomas, Formby

53

Most photographers would have avoided such a massive range of contrast between the shadow and the sunshine. Thank goodness the Williamsons did not. They have epitomised the beauty of a Westmorland evening.

EVENING
D. C. & S. J. Williamson, Burton-in-Kendal

19:00

I once asked a shepherd how many cuts it took to shear a sheep. 'You're not supposed to cut 'em', he said. Quite. Shearing such valuable animals demands skill and concentration, and the picture shows both.

SHEARING
S. A. Walker, Brindle

54

 THE BOOT   `19:25`
Wayne Nesbeth, Cheetham Hill

Good close-up photography requires observation, imagination and ability. Wayne had all three so he didn't put his foot in it!

Here is an intriguing and impressionistic still that is full of movement, taken at a travelling fair. John Wesson used a zoom lens with a burst of flash during a slow shutter speed. And if you think that's easy, try it.

▼   RUNCORN FAIR   `20:00`
John Wesson, Liverpool

55

EVENING AT WALSHAW
Adrian Ashurst, Walshaw

The picture is remarkable on two counts: as landscape photography it is close to perfection; and who would expect to find such beauty in industrial Lancashire? Well, I would; but then I was brought up there.

▲ **DANCE CLASS**
Jenny Young, Farnworth

`20:05`

According to Jenny Young, the dancers have their handclasp all wrong. Not that they look too upset about it. After all, one goes to dance classes to get it right, sooner or later.

What a classy piece of sports photography this is. Aidan's flashgun has trapped the action during a slow exposure, and the blurred background gives an exciting impression of speed.

▼ **ON YER BIKE**
Aidan Nuttall, Macclesfield

`20:10`

20:08

An historic moment at the Hampton Road United Reformed Church in Southport; the scene reminds me of my chapel-based childhood. It is timeless. It is the modern microphone which tells us that faith abounds, even in the nineteen-nineties.

PASTOR'S INDUCTION
Mrs C. P. W. Brown, Southport

20:15

I do like a happy picture. Stuart had taken the early bath from Norweb in Preston, and his workmates are obviously fond of him. They saw him off at Tiggis in Preston, and Gill took a splendid snap.

STUART'S RETIREMENT
Gill Brown, Leyland

WHEELTON'S BOBBY
David Coan, Chorley

David finished his tea and told his wife, "I'm just off to Top Lock at Wheelton". The bobby came whizzing round the corner as he arrived and his camera was ready. That's how you take winning pictures.

59

This is the traditional North West which thrives in the
moorland villages around Saddleworth. You can almost hear
the music in this superb picture. Superb enough to show us that
they are playing a section of Mussorgsky's 'Pictures at the
Exhibition'. How appropriate!

 BAND PRACTICE
Keith Buckley, Mossley

20:30

He's a barefoot skier as it happens, which might explain that dramatic spray. David was invited into the boat when he told them why he was taking pictures, and a golden opportunity produced a winner.

DEE SKIER
David Buckley, Connah's Quay

61

21:25

Another slice of the traditional North West which demanded to be included. The picture is a fine example of available light black and white photography. It was taken on a traditional camera, too – a Leica M2.

CHIPPY
M. T. Bentley, Littleborough

21:45

Sheila's picture of domestic bliss caused more oohs and aahs than any other picture in the competition. It is a charming study, and deserves far wider viewing than it will get in the Coyle family album.

CALUM AND TOTO
Sheila Coyle, Wigan

22:00

Lots of dockside atmosphere in this very good night scene. It says a lot for the light-gathering properties of modern films, too. At one time you would have had to give an impossibly long time-exposure.

ALBERT DOCK
Mrs J. McLeod, Liverpool

22:45

This is simply an excellent conversation piece. It has captured vivid expressions at an after-show party for the Swinton Drama Group. They had just performed 'Daisy pulls it off'. Mrs Pierce-Jones pulled off a great shot.

DRAMA GROUP
Mrs C. M. Pierce-Jones, Middleton

63

24:00

And Robin Sharples produced the final picture of a memorable day. What could be more representative of the region than the Victorian opulence of Rochdale's Town Hall and its clock. Thank you, and goodnight. And so to bed.

 ROCHDALE TOWN HALL
Robin Sharples, Rossendale